Dalon Wayne Williams
from Bruce Alexander Williams
Christmas 2009.

HISTORIC PHOTOS OF
UNIVERSITY OF
ALABAMA FOOTBALL

TEXT AND CAPTIONS BY JOSEPH WOODRUFF

TURNER
PUBLISHING COMPANY

On Thanksgiving Day 1915, Bully Vandegraaff played his final game at Alabama. He kicked a field goal and six extra points as Alabama defeated Ole Miss 53–0 at Rickwood Field in Birmingham.

HISTORIC PHOTOS OF
UNIVERSITY OF
ALABAMA FOOTBALL

Turner Publishing Company
200 4th Avenue North • Suite 950
Nashville, Tennessee 37219
(615) 255-2665

www.turnerpublishing.com

Historic Photos of University of Alabama Football

Copyright © 2009 Turner Publishing Company

Library of Congress Control Number: 2009921192

ISBN-13: 978-1-59652-530-6

Printed in China

09 10 11 12 13 14 15—0 9 8 7 6 5 4 3 2 1

CONTENTS

Alabama students form a letter A on the field prior to a home game around 1920.

ACKNOWLEDGMENTS

This volume, *Historic Photos of University of Alabama Football,* is the result of the cooperation and efforts of many individuals, organizations, and corporations. It is with great thanks that we acknowledge the valuable contribution of the following for their generous support:

Paul W. Bryant Museum, The University of Alabama
The W. S. Hoole Special Collections Library, The University of Alabama

The writer wishes to acknowledge the invaluable contributions of J. Wade Woodruff. No author could have a better research assistant, and no father could have a better son.

———————

With the exception of touching up imperfections that have accrued with the passage of time and cropping where necessary, no changes have been made to the photographs. The focus and clarity of many images is limited by the technology and the ability of the photographer at the time they were taken.

PREFACE

Between November 11, 1892, and February 22, 1893, students at the University of Alabama played the school's first official season of football. Alabama played one game against a collection of Birmingham-area high school students, and two games against the Birmingham Athletic Club. They took a record of two wins and one loss into the final contest against Auburn.

Alabama lost.

From these humble beginnings, the Alabama football program grew to become the standard-bearer for college football in the South, bursting upon the national scene with an improbable defeat of the formidable Quakers from the University of Pennsylvania in 1922, and placing an exclamation point next to its claim to be a national power with its come-from-behind Rose Bowl victory over Washington on New Year's Day 1926. The Crimson Tide would become the cornerstone program of the Southeastern Conference and achieve further greatness as it accumulated championships in gaudy numbers and established bone-deep rivalries with its counterparts in Tennessee, Georgia, and Mississippi.

Scores of players and coaches brought Alabama's football program from its humble origins as a club sport to its stature as the leading football power in the South and a coequal of the best in the nation. In 1915, W. T. "Bully" Vandegraaff became the first Alabama player to be named a college All-American. Twenty members of the College Football Hall of Fame are associated with the University of Alabama; half of them played for or coached the Crimson Tide during its first golden age—including Don Hutson, Millard "Dixie" Howell, Johnny Mack Brown, Allison T. S. "Pooley" Hubert, and Paul W. "Bear" Bryant. Under the coaching of Xen Scott, Alabama became the first southern football team to win a game played north of the Mason-Dixon Line. Death prevented Scott from coaching Alabama to its first national championship. That feat would be achieved by his successor, the great Wallace Wade, who won three—in 1925, 1926, and 1930.

If the list of the fathers of Alabama's football success had to be narrowed to a single person, there is no reasonable debate that it would be George Hutcheson Denny.

A native Virginian, the son of a Presbyterian minister, a Latin scholar, and the youngest man ever to be named president of Washington and Lee University, Denny may not have appeared to be a person who could build a college football program into a national power. But, as president of the University of Alabama, he understood the role that a successful football program could play in helping a university achieve national exposure and grow. During his 25-year tenure, the university's enrollment increased from barely 400 to more than 5,000. He hired four head coaches—Thomas Kelley, Xen Scott, Wallace Wade, and Frank Thomas. Their combined record during Denny's presidency was 155-35-10 and included three national and six conference championships.

The 1950s would see the second act of Alabama's football story, as the once proud program sank first into mediocrity and finally into incompetence. Alabama's rivals feasted on what remained of a team and tradition that had brashly placed a southern stamp on the premier sport of college athletics.

All great stories have a third act, and the curtain rose on the greatest era of Alabama football with the return to Tuscaloosa of Paul W. Bryant, a former player who would transform Alabama football almost as if reinventing the game itself. In the span of history covered by this book, Alabama won 18 Southeastern Conference championships. Bryant coached 13 of them. From its first national title following the 1925 season, to Bryant's retirement after the 1982 campaign, Alabama won 11 national championships. Bryant was at the helm for 6 of them. Over that same span of time, Alabama achieved 14 undefeated regular seasons. Bryant was the head coach for half of them. If the Rose Bowl win in 1926 marked the beginning of the first golden age for Tide football, that epoch was but a prelude for the unparalleled success Alabama would know in its second golden age under Bryant.

This book does not pretend to be an encyclopedic history of Alabama football. Rather, it is an attempt to tell the Alabama story, from its beginnings through the end of the Bryant era, in pictures more than words. It is an effort to present the history of Alabama football through images of artistic value, and thereby explore, through the medium of photography, the intangible qualities that make the sport of college football as played by the University of Alabama an enterprise of surpassing joy for those who are devoted to and inspired by it.

—Joseph Woodruff

Fans in Tuscaloosa chartered a special train for the trip to Birmingham on November 5, 1917, to see Alabama play Sewanee (the University of the South).

The Origins of Greatness

(1892–1922)

Football was introduced to the University of Alabama by William G. Little, a native of Livingston, Alabama, who fell in love with the game while enrolled at Phillips Exeter Academy in Andover, Massachusetts. In 1892, Little organized the squad that played the university's first-ever season, and he served as team captain. Thirty-four years later, and by then the probate judge of his home county, he organized a celebratory reception for the national champion Crimson Tide, fresh from its Rose Bowl victory over Washington, as the team made one of many whistle-stops on its railroad journey from Pasadena, California, to Tuscaloosa.

Fourteen men served as head coach during the first three decades of Alabama football. Their combined record of achievement can charitably be described as uneven. Eli Abbot, a former player, coached four seasons over a span of ten years for a record of only 7-13. J. W. H. Pollard coached a single season, 1906, but had a respectable record of 5-1. For the three seasons between 1907 and 1909, the official record book does not identify anyone as head coach. D. V. Graves' overall record was 21-12-3, and he never coached a losing season; but he was winless against Sewanee, and he left after the 1914 season. George Denny hired Thomas Kelley to replace Graves. Because of World War I, college football play was suspended in 1918. When play resumed in 1919, Denny replaced Kelley with Xen Scott.

Scott had no résumé as a football coach when he was hired for the 1919 season, but what he lacked in credentials, he more than made up for in results. The first team he coached achieved a record of 8-1-0, at the time Alabama's best ever, and his 1920 squad eclipsed that mark by winning 10 games. Scott's four Alabama teams averaged nearly 30 points per game and held opponents scoreless in 20 of the 41 games they played. His 1922 team shocked the college football establishment by traveling to Philadelphia and beating the physically superior powerhouse team from the University of Pennsylvania.

When Scott died after the 1922 season, President Denny again hired someone with no head-coaching experience, and in Wallace Wade, Denny found the right man to complete the journey on the path of greatness Xen Scott had charted.

Livingston, Alabama, native William G. Little brought the game of football to Tuscaloosa from Phillips Exeter Academy in Andover, Massachusetts. Thirty-seven years after his last collegiate game, Little was present for the dedication of Alabama's first on-campus stadium. His son, also named William G. Little, played for Alabama in 1920 and 1921.

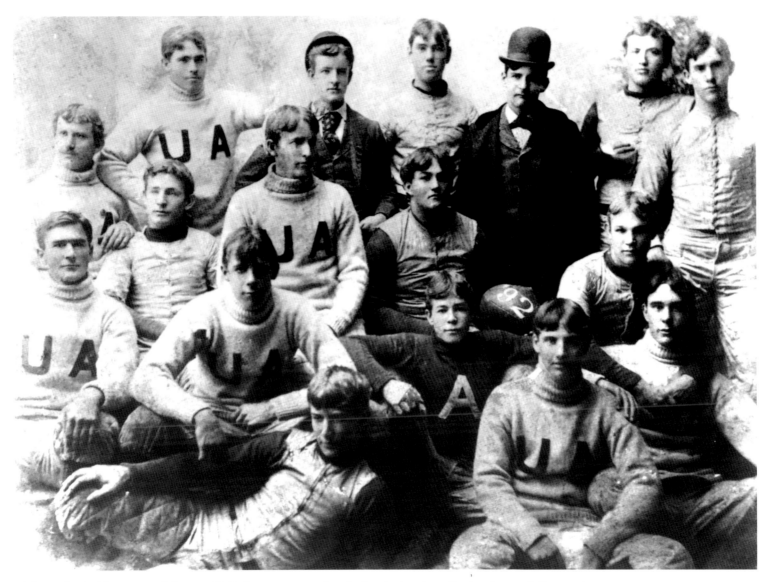

Alabama football began as a club sport. E. B. Beaumont, wearing the bowler hat, is credited as the team's first coach. His one-season career record was 2-2-0.

Shown here, the first touchdown in the history of the great Alabama-Auburn football rivalry was scored by Auburn, which went on to win the game by a score of 40–16. What later became known as the Iron Bowl was first played at Lakeview Park in Birmingham before a crowd of 5,000 on February 22, 1893. One hundred and five years after that first meeting, Auburn and Alabama would play in Tuscaloosa before a crowd in excess of 92,000.

The intensity of the Alabama-Auburn rivalry was evident from the inaugural game in February 1893. According to the official recap, Auburn scored one of its touchdowns on a 65-yard end run, after which "It required several minutes to clear the field."

Games between Auburn and Alabama, initiated in February 1893, were suspended for 41 years after 1907 because of a financial dispute. The series was only resumed in 1948 after the Alabama legislature required the schools to play as a condition of receiving public funding.

The 1893 team was the first to play a school from outside the state of Alabama. The University of the South, located in Sewanee, Tennessee (and popularly known as Sewanee), defeated Alabama 20–0. When the two teams met a year later, at Birmingham's Lakeview Park on November 15, 1894, Alabama prevailed over Sewanee 24–4. According to the official archives, "The game passed off quietly with two exceptions, Abbott [an Alabama player who later coached the team] was put out of the game for striking another player and Alabama complained about the officiating."

Alabama's football team was originally known as the Cadets, an acknowledgment of the school's origins as a military academy. That name, however, quickly gave way to two other names that preceded Crimson Tide: the Varsity, and the Crimson White. The 1900 team is shown here.

Another early name for the team, the Thin Red Line, was widely used until 1906. The 1901 version of the Thin Red Line is shown here.

Alabama occasionally played games at Lakeview Park in Birmingham, including a 6–6 tie against Tennessee on November 28, 1901. The official account of the game reports "The game was called on account of darkness when a crowd of 2,000 spectators rushed on the field in protest of a decision by umpire Payne." The lack of adequate crowd control at Lakeview Park no doubt contributed to the decision in 1910 to move games played in Birmingham to Rickwood Field.

These fans of the 1907 Alabama team witnessed a 6–6 tie against Auburn, the last game between the two schools for 41 years.

Guy Lowman's record in 1910, his only season as head football coach, was 4-4-0. In each of its four losses, Alabama failed to score.

This photograph of the 1910 team was taken on the Quadrangle at a spot not very far from where Denny Chimes, the bell tower dedicated to university president George H. Denny, would eventually be built.

The rosters of early football teams were fairly small. Frequently, only the bare minimum of 11 players would be on the squad. Former players who served as assistant coaches and managers wore the letter sweaters they earned in their playing days.

For 16 years, Alabama played its Birmingham "home" games at Rickwood Field. In 1926, Birmingham's Municipal Stadium (later renamed Legion Field) was completed, and for the next 70 years, Alabama played most of its high-profile home games in that venerable structure that called itself the "Football Capitol of the South."

D. V. Graves (far right) coached Alabama for four seasons, 1911–1914. His Alabama teams outscored their opponents 708 to 190.

D. V. Graves (standing with hands on hips) supervises practice. Alabama played Ole Miss in Tuscaloosa on November 8, 1912. The official summary of the game, a 10–9 Alabama victory, describes it as "one of the most spectacular games ever staged on the Alabama campus."

Hargrove, Adrian, and youngest brother W. T. "Bully" Vandegraaff were teammates in 1912. The next year Hargrove was the team captain. The three brothers are pictured here on the Quadrangle, with Toumey Hall visible in the background.

The 1912 team, like most of its predecessors, played its on-campus games on the Quadrangle. Spectators stood or sat in makeshift bleachers. George Denny knew that in order for the football program to improve, a better venue than the Quadrangle had to be found for home games.

The Alabama backfield of 1912 poses in a representation of the T formation. Quarterback Farley Moody holds the ball.
Next to Moody, Holt McDowell joins two of the trio of Vandegraaff brothers, Hargrove and Adrian.

In this photo of the 1912 team, Farley Moody wears the white letter sweater of the team captain. Coach D. V. Graves stands at far right. Graves customarily wore his letter sweater from his playing days at Missouri.

Team captain Farley Moody (center) stands with Alabama head coach D. V. Graves (left) and an unidentified third individual. Moody would be killed in action in France one month before the armistice ending World War I. He lies buried in Tuscaloosa literally in the shadows of Bryant-Denny Stadium, in a cemetery adjacent to what is now Bryant Drive.

The youngest Vandegraaff brother, Bully, closing to tackle a Tulane ball carrier, was the first Alabama player to be named an All-American.

Prior to the 1909 season, a field goal only counted for two points, and a touchdown only earned four. By the time Bully Vandegraaff was kicking for Alabama, the scoring had been adjusted to its present three points for a field goal.

Despite his teams having amassed a point total better than three times that of their opponents, D. V. Graves' winning percentage was only .583, and in four seasons he never defeated Sewanee.

The 1914 team posted a season record of 5-4-0. D. V. Graves' final game, December 2, 1914, was a 20–3 loss to the Carlisle Indian Industrial School, coached by Pop Warner.

With football in its third decade at the university, students were finding ways to enhance the game-day experience.
One of the earliest photos of an Alabama marching band, this one dates to 1914.

George Denny's first major improvement to the university's football facilities was the 1915 construction of University Field, located in an open area south of a classroom building named after Alabama's first team captain, W. G. Little. The team played 14 seasons at this site and compiled a home-field record of 43-2, holding its opponents scoreless in 35 of those games.

By the time the 1915 Alabama squad took the field, the team was being called the Crimson Tide. Credit for the name goes to Hugh Roberts, sports editor of the *Birmingham Age-Herald* in 1907, who used it to describe Alabama's play against Auburn in the 6–6 tie game that was the last between the two schools before the rivalry took its 41-year hiatus.

Despite the improvements offered by University Field as successor to the Quadrangle, Alabama had no permanent football facility on campus until 1929. In order to play before sizable crowds of paying fans, Alabama had to travel to venues such as Birmingham's Rickwood Field, where this 1915 game took place.

Bully Vandegraaff kicks a field goal in 1915.

Here Bully Vandegraaff punts the ball at Rickwood Field.

The drop kick was a standard play in football's early years. Eventually the ball was reshaped in a more aerodynamic fashion, and the forward pass came into use.

The Sewanee Tigers were arguably the South's best college team in the years before World War I and became a charter member of the Southeastern Conference in 1931. The school was a regular opponent of Alabama and dominated the series in its early years. Alabama could muster only one win (1894) over the first 11 games. Even with all three Vandegraaff brothers on his team, D. V. Graves could do no better than a tie in 1912.

Coach Xen Scott's first Alabama team, the 1919 squad, had a season record of 8-1-0 and only gave up 22 points all season. Seven of Alabama's wins were shutouts. The team's only loss, by four points, was to Vanderbilt.

Scott's 1920 varsity team was the first in school history to win 10 games in a season and outscored all opponents 377–35. Eight of its wins were shutouts.

Alabama kicks off at Rickwood Field.

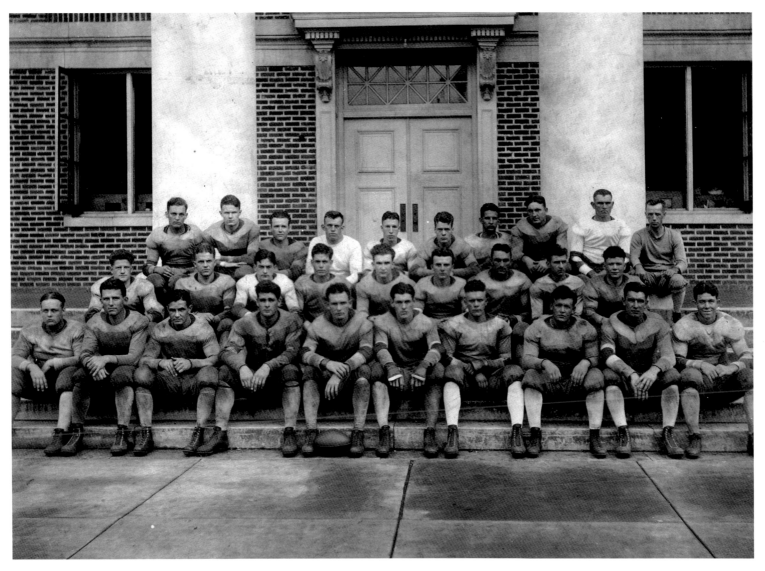

In 1922 Alabama became the first southern college to win a football game played north of the Mason-Dixon Line when it defeated the University of Pennsylvania in Philadelphia. Sportswriter Grantland Rice predicted the game against Alabama would be a "breather" for the Quakers. Alabama stunned the crowd of 25,000 by beating the physically larger Penn team 9–7. Southern sportswriters hailed the Alabama win as a long-delayed reckoning for the Confederacy's loss at Gettysburg.

Pooley Hubert, carrying the ball, was a 20-year-old freshman on the 1922 team. During the Penn game he fumbled while crossing the Quaker goal line, but the fumble was recovered by Alabama's Shorty Probst for a touchdown. Alabama's victory over Penn was celebrated throughout the South. In Tuscaloosa, the score was painted on the exterior wall of a downtown drugstore, where it remained a visible tribute for over 20 years.

A TRADITION OF GREATNESS

(1923–1946)

Alabama's rise to national prominence was completed on January 1, 1926, with its improbable win over Washington in the Rose Bowl. The upset victory resulted in the first of three national championships that Wallace Wade won in only eight seasons as Alabama's head football coach. Wade's Alabama teams shut out their opponents in nearly two-thirds of the 77 games he coached, including a 24–0 bludgeoning of Washington State in the Rose Bowl on New Year's Day 1931. His 1925 team allowed only a single touchdown the entire regular season. The 1926 Rose Bowl win was evidently regarded as no fluke, because Alabama paid a return visit to Pasadena the next year, and, despite a 7–7 tie with Stanford, won a second national championship.

With the 1930 national championship, its third in six seasons, Alabama took its place as an equal of the elite programs in the sport and forever changed national perceptions of the quality of play of college football in the South. But the 1931 Rose Bowl was the last game Wade would coach the Tide.

In Frank Thomas, Alabama acquired a coach able to sustain the greatness achieved by Wallace Wade. Only Paul Bryant, a Thomas pupil, would serve a longer tenure than Thomas as Alabama's head football coach. Thomas achieved a winning percentage of .812 and captured six conference and two national championships. Three times, Thomas' Alabama teams ran winning streaks to 14 games, and from November 4, 1933, through October 5, 1935, Alabama did not lose a single game. Of Thomas' 115 wins at Alabama, 62 were shutouts. In the 1933 season, Thomas' defense held all opponents to a mere 17 points. Seven of the players he coached were later inducted into the College Football Hall of Fame.

Thomas was the first coach to take a team to all four of the major college bowls of that era: Rose, Cotton, Orange, and Sugar. He coached Alabama in three Rose Bowl games—including the school's final Rose Bowl appearance, on New Year's Day 1946, a 34–14 drubbing of the University of Southern California.

After the 1946 season, Frank Thomas retired from the coaching profession, having established football greatness as an institutional tradition and bringing to a close the first golden age of Alabama football.

George H. Denny understood the importance of athletic excellence. When he became president of the University of Alabama in 1911, the student enrollment was barely 400, and through 18 seasons of football Alabama had only been able to manage a winning record 9 times. When Denny retired 25 years later, Alabama's enrollment was over 5,000, and the Tide never experienced a losing season during his presidency.

The potential for greatness that Xen Scott established at Alabama was realized by his successor, Wallace Wade, who would win three national championships and compile a record of 61-13-3.

In his three seasons as head coach, from 1915 to 1917, Thomas Kelley turned the tables on Sewanee and accumulated a record of 2-0-1 against the team known as the Iron Men. Xen Scott's teams beat Sewanee in 1919 and 1920, lost in 1921, and played to a 7–7 tie in the signature year of 1922. Here in 1923, Wallace Wade's first Alabama team beat Sewanee 7–0. His and Frank Thomas' teams played Sewanee 12 times and never lost.

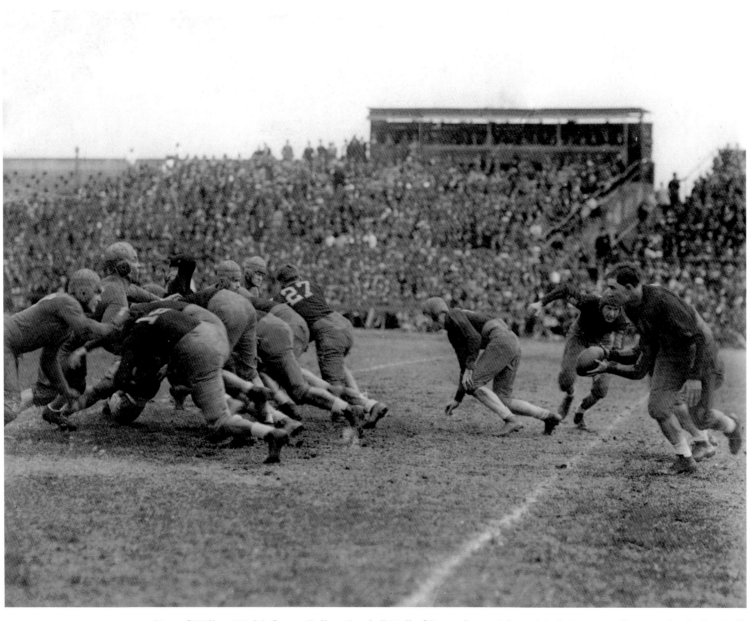

Two of Wallace Wade's future College Football Hall of Fame players, Johnny Mack Brown (pulling to take the handoff) and Pooley Hubert (playing without a helmet) are shown in action against Georgia at Rickwood Field in 1925, the year Alabama won its first national championship.

Southern football was lightly regarded by the powerhouse programs and the newspaper writers who covered them. Almost by default, Alabama was asked to play in the 1926 Rose Bowl game, after more prominent eastern schools declined the invitation. Despite an impressive undefeated regular season, which saw the Tide shut out eight opponents and yield only a single touchdown, the Washington Huskies were expected to make short work of the team from Alabama, shown here at breakfast in the Garden of Roses in Pasadena.

With good reason, Coach Wade worried that his unsophisticated players would be distracted by the numerous diversions available in Pasadena, so he scheduled workouts at stops during the four-day train journey to California, imposed a strict curfew, and ran some of the toughest practices of the season after the team arrived on the West Coast.

The practices that Coach Wade ran prior to the Rose Bowl game were among the most rigorous of the season.

The 1926 Rose Bowl game was much more than an opportunity for the University of Alabama to win a national championship in football. People throughout the South considered the game to be a chance for redemption. Alabama's biggest promoter, Champ Pickens (at right with cigar), wired the presidents of civic clubs throughout the region asking their members to send telegrams of support and encouragement to the Tide players. Perusing the pregame news with Pickens are graduate manager V. Hugo Friedman and "chief rooter" Cecil Grimes.

Many years later, Clyde Bolton of the *Birmingham News* would write, "The 1926 Rose Bowl was without a doubt the most important game before or since in Southern football history."

Wallace Wade, coaching on the sidelines at the Rose Bowl, January 1, 1926, was the first person ever to participate in the venerated bowl game as both a player (Brown, 1916) and coach (Alabama, 1926, 1927, 1931).

The Huskies scored touchdowns in both the first and second quarters, but missed the extra points, to take a 12–0 lead into the locker room at halftime of the 1926 Rose Bowl. Wallace Wade reportedly made only one statement to his players at the half: "And they told me southern boys would fight." It was all the men in crimson needed to hear. They scored three touchdowns in the third period. Here, Pooley Hubert runs off tackle for a 12-yard gain.

Pooley Hubert scored Alabama's first touchdown against Washington after five consecutive carries. The Crimson Tide's second touchdown came on a 65-yard pass from Hubert to Johnny Mack Brown.

Johnny Mack Brown scored his second touchdown, Alabama's third, before the end of the third period on a five-yard run. The Huskies rallied for a fourth-quarter touchdown, but the missed extra points in the first half were the difference in the 1926 Rose Bowl, as Alabama stunned the nation by upsetting the heavily favored Huskies 20–19.

Throughout the South, Alabama's Rose Bowl victory was celebrated by jubilant crowds. The team train was greeted at every whistle-stop as it made its way back to Tuscaloosa, where these fans and a newsreel crew awaited the champions. The Crimson Tide's stunning victory was a cultural watershed. Historian Andrew Doyle writes that it was "a sublime tonic for Southerners . . . buffeted by a legacy of defeat . . . , poverty, and isolation from the American political and cultural mainstream."

Wade (right), seen here with some of his assistants, was known as a perfectionist. His College Football Hall of Fame biography quotes him as saying "The best you can do is not enough if it doesn't get the job done." In his career at Alabama, he mentored assistant coaches Jess Neely, Hank Crisp, and Bully Vandegraaff, among others.

In Pasadena, Tide players participate in a drill during practice for the 1927 Rose Bowl. The only thing Alabama could do to equal its remarkable achievement of winning the 1925 national championship was to win it again in 1926. From November 1924 to October 1927, Alabama did not lose a game.

Alabama's 7–7 tie with Stanford in the 1927 Rose Bowl marked the 21st game in a row that Alabama went undefeated. The streak would eventually reach 24 games and include two national championships.

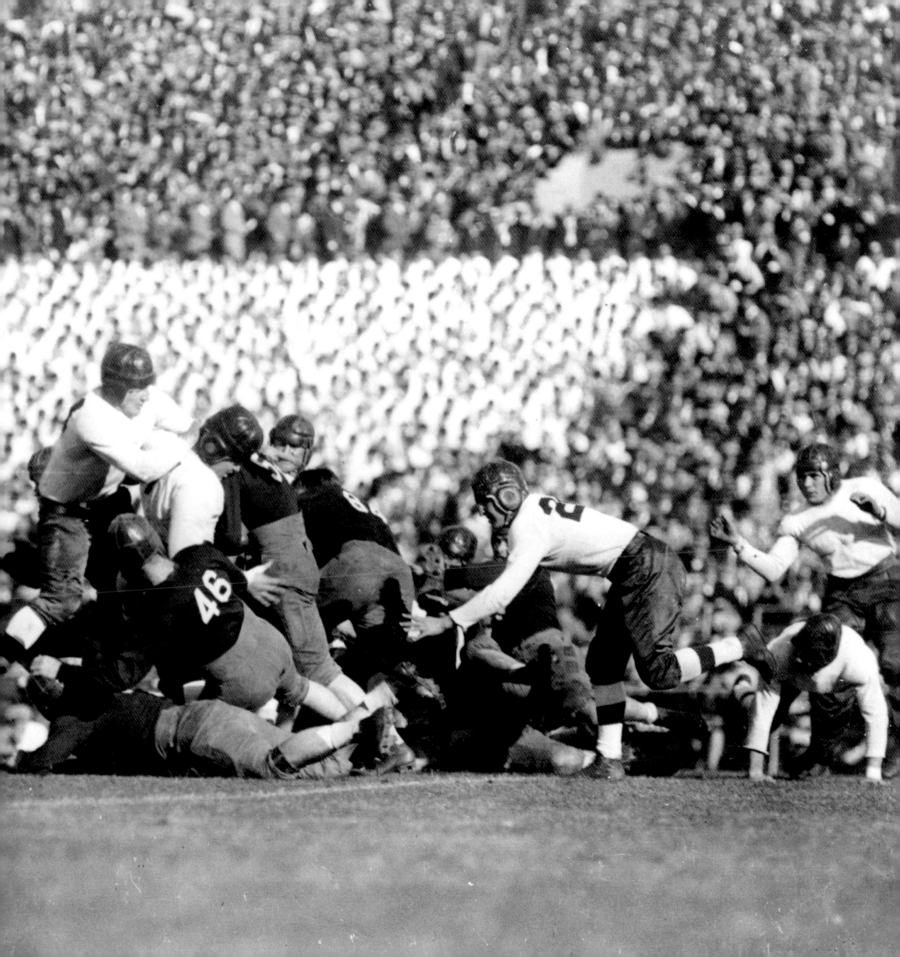

George Denny's quest to improve the university's athletic facilities was realized with the construction of a permanent on-campus stadium. Denny Stadium was dedicated at the 1929 homecoming game by Governor Bibb Graves. In attendance among the capacity crowd of 12,000 was Alabama's first team captain, William G. Little.

On May 27, 1929, Governor Bibb Graves officiated at the dedication of Denny Chimes. Students and alumni raised the $40,000 needed to build Denny Chimes. Fund-raising was spurred by fears that Denny was considering resigning his position as president of the university to return to his home state of Virginia.

The 1930 edition of the Crimson Tide, the last team Wallace Wade coached at Alabama, may have been his best. That season, Alabama outscored all opponents 271–13. Eight of its ten games were shutouts, including a 24–0 pounding of Washington State in the Rose Bowl, a game that was over at the half, with Alabama leading 21–0.

The 1930 team, pictured outside the athletic dormitory, set a varsity record for scoring defense—13 points allowed in 10 games—that will likely never be broken. The 1933 team came closest, with 17 points allowed in 9 games.

Five of the 18 Alabama players to be inducted into the College Football Hall of Fame—Johnny Mack Brown, Johnny Cain, Frank Howard, Pooley Hubert, and Fred Sington—played at least one season for Coach Wade. Here, Johnny Mack Brown can be seen standing, hands on hips, to the left of Wade.

Before the 1931 Rose Bowl, Coach Wade (far left), university officials, and selected senior players, including Fred Sington (second row left, in letter sweater), were entertained at some of Pasadena's finer dining establishments. If the good food and fellowship were calculated by Pacific Conference partisans to undermine Alabama's preparations for the game against the unbeaten Washington State Cougars, the ploy didn't work.

Alabama's team captain, Charles Clement, and his Washington State counterpart join the reigning Festival of Roses queen at midfield prior to the 1931 Rose Bowl game.

Alabama's quarterback, Monk Campbell, only completed two passes against Washington State in the 1931 Rose Bowl—one for 36 yards, the other for 62 yards and a touchdown. Alabama intercepted the Cougar quarterback three times and outrushed WSU 261 yards to 145.

Alabama quarterback Monk Campbell also handled placekicking duties. Pictured here is one of his three successful extra point kicks in the second quarter of the 1931 Rose Bowl.

In the Rose Bowl's earliest years, the opposing teams divided the gate receipts and left Pasadena with thousands of dollars in cash. After the 1931 game, in the depths of the Great Depression, George Denny (left) brought Alabama's sizable share back to Tuscaloosa, where he used it to redeem scrip that had been issued to members of the university faculty.

Fred Sington is among Alabama's most renowned student athletes. During his four seasons playing tackle, the Tide had a winning percentage of .717, and the team captured both the Southern Conference (a precursor of the Southeastern Conference) championship and the national championship his senior year.

Fred Sington (driving) was the president of the Alabama student body during the 1930–1931 academic year.

Not only was Fred Sington a four-year player on the varsity football team, he also excelled at baseball, basketball, and track.

Sington's intellect was equal to his athletic prowess. In his senior year at the Capstone, he was inducted into the Phi Beta Kappa academic honor society on Honors Day.

After graduating from Alabama, Sington played nine years of professional baseball, including seasons in the major leagues with the Washington Senators and Brooklyn Dodgers. Upon U.S. entry into World War II, he left baseball for active duty in the Navy, where he rose to the rank of lieutenant commander.

Wallace Wade's decision to leave Alabama, after winning his third national championship in eight years, to coach football at Duke stunned the Tide football community and forced George Denny to hire the fourth head coach of his tenure as university president. He chose wisely by hiring Frank Thomas. Here, some years later, Wade and Thomas reenact the handoff.

Frank Thomas' first Alabama team (1931) lost only one game and outscored its opponents 360–57.

Against Tennessee in 1931, future College Football Hall of Famer Johnny "Hurri" Cain punted 19 times for an average of 48 yards per kick.

As a sophomore quarterback in 1930, Johnny Cain was the only starter who was not a senior. The next year, Frank Thomas moved Cain to fullback. He made the All-Southern list at both positions. Birmingham sportswriter Zipp Newman wrote of Cain: "He could run, block, punt, and play defense, the best all-around back I ever saw."

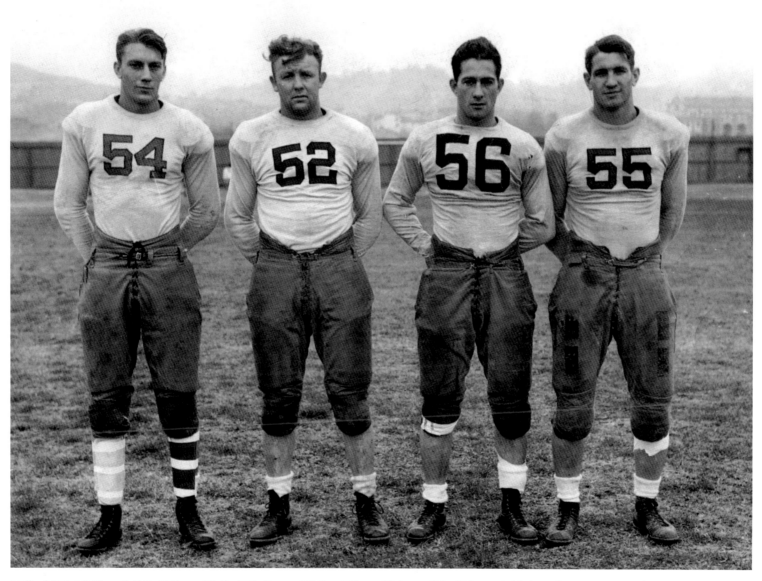

Millard "Dixie" Howell (54), Hillman Holly (52), Jimmy Walker (56), and Johnny Cain (55) stand side by side in 1932. Howell and Cain are members of the College Football Hall of Fame.

Alabama's fourth national championship was won by the 1934 team coached by Frank Thomas (in the dark suit). The Tide capped a perfect season with a 29–13 Rose Bowl victory over Stanford. That win, on New Year's Day 1935, was Alabama's 14th in a row, dating back to November 4, 1933. Here, Thomas and two of his stars, Don Hutson (left) and Dixie Howell (right), greet USC coach Howard Jones.

In an era devoted to power running and field position, Alabama and Stanford combined for an unexpected 36 passing attempts in the 1935 Rose Bowl. Alabama outgained Stanford through the air 216 yards to 86, and intercepted the Indians four times. Tide quarterback Dixie Howell, shown here, accounted for 313 all-purpose yards.

Dixie Howell is shown scoring the first of his two rushing touchdowns, on a five-yard run, in the 1935 Rose Bowl against Stanford. His second touchdown came on a run of 65 yards. His two scoring runs were part of a 22-point explosion by Alabama in the second quarter.

The celebrations that hailed Alabama on its return from the West Coast in January 1935 were reminiscent of those that greeted the university's first national championship team in January 1926.

Don Hutson practically
invented the modern
position of wide receiver.
His six receptions for 165
yards and two touchdowns
in the 1935 Rose Bowl
victory over Stanford
was a harbinger of even
greater achievements as a
professional. He finished
his pro career with 488
receptions; the next-best
player at the time had only
188. Hutson once said,
"For every pass I caught
in a game, I caught a
thousand in practice."

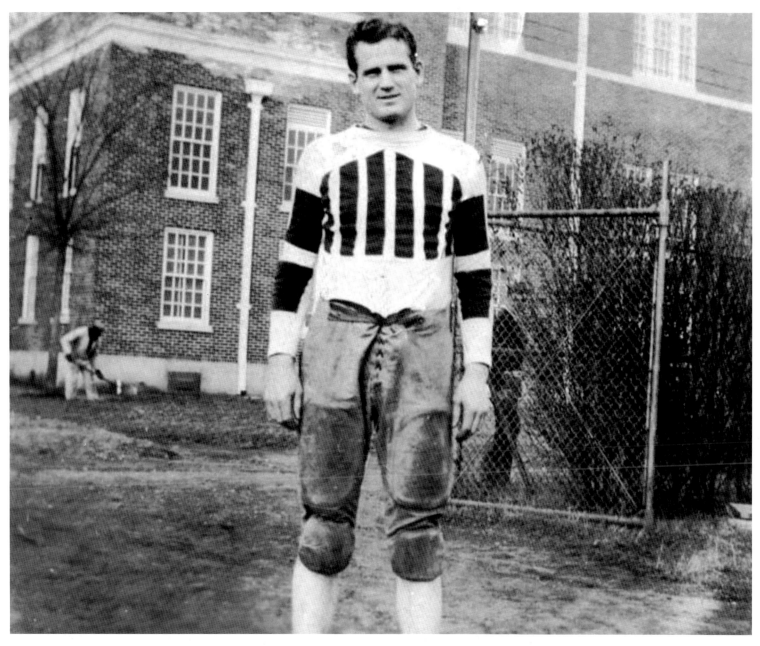

Two of Dixie Howell's passes in the 1935 Rose Bowl were completed to this player, referred to at the time merely as the "other end" opposite Don Hutson—Paul Bryant.

Paul Bryant was one of Coach Frank Thomas' most successful pupils. Not only did Bryant play for Thomas, he also began his own coaching career—one of the greatest of all time in the profession—as an assistant on Thomas' staff at Alabama.

The 1934 offensive line: (left to right) Paul Bryant, Bill Lee, Bob Ed Morrow, Kavanaugh Francis, Charlie Marr, James Whatley, and Don Hutson.

Riley "General" Smith was one of five players coached by Frank Thomas to be inducted into the College Football Hall of Fame. He played on the 1934 national championship team that beat Stanford in the Rose Bowl. The second player taken in the first professional football draft, Smith had an outstanding career with the Boston Redskins.

During festivities prior to the 1938 Rose Bowl game, a young Ronald Reagan interviewed some of the Alabama players. Reagan, who had played football as a student at Eureka College, was working as a radio announcer while auditioning for film roles. Seated at far left, Leroy Monsky, Alabama's center, is wearing a bandage over his left eye, the result of an injury sustained in practice. The Rose Bowl itself proved a disappointment, as the undefeated Crimson Tide was shut out by California, 13–0.

A three-year player for Frank Thomas, Holt Rast earned All-American honors in 1941, his senior year.

Holt Rast (45) was Alabama's leading receiver in the school's national championship season of 1941. In later years he served with distinction in the Alabama legislature, was a successful businessman, and became one of the founders of the Alabama Sports Hall of Fame.

Holt Rast served in the U.S. Army during the Second World War. He was twice wounded in action and was decorated with the Silver Star for valor in combat.

Shown here in 1945, the elephant became the Tide mascot after a sportswriter drew a comparison between the beasts and Alabama's linemen, who were physically larger than the opposing team's players.

Frank Thomas (center) was the first person to coach a team in all four of the major bowl games of his era: Cotton, Orange, Sugar, and Rose. He did so in four consecutive seasons: 1941, 1942, 1944, and 1945 (the 1943 season was suspended due to World War II). Thomas' record through those bowl games was 3-1. He led Alabama to a national championship in 1941 and a perfect season in 1945. Jimmy Nelson (left) scored two touchdowns, one on a 72-yard punt return, in Alabama's 29–21 win over Texas A&M in the 1942 Cotton Bowl, and was voted MVP of the game. Holt Rast (right) returned an interception for a touchdown in Thomas' 1942 Cotton Bowl victory.

Frank Thomas coached Alabama for more seasons (15) than any head coach other than Paul Bryant. During his tenure with the Tide, he coached seven men later inducted into the College Football Hall of Fame. Two of those were teammates Harry Gilmer (left) and Vaughn Mancha (right).

Vaughn Mancha
played every snap on
offense, defense, and
special teams—a full 60
minutes of football—in
the January 1, 1945,
Sugar Bowl.

Harry Gilmer's 2,894 career passing yards and 26 career touchdown passes stood as Alabama records for more than 20 years.

In his career, Harry Gilmer rushed for 1,673 yards and 24 touchdowns. He added 4 more touchdowns in punt, kick, and interception returns. Combined with his 26 touchdown passes, he set a school record of 54 career touchdowns scored or thrown that has yet to be equaled.

At the conclusion of the 1945 regular season, Harry Gilmer, Frank Thomas, and Vaughn Mancha were able to wonder whether Alabama would play in the Sugar, Rose, or Orange Bowl. It turned out to be the Rose Bowl. Alabama defeated USC 34–14 in the 1946 Rose Bowl, the last one played before the New Year's Day classic became limited to teams from the Pacific and Big Ten conferences.

Pregame festivities and events leading up to the 1946 Rose Bowl did not distract players like Vaughn Mancha (second from right) and Harry Gilmer (right) from the task of beating USC.

Tom Whitley (43) represented Alabama at the coin toss for the 1946 Rose Bowl. It proved to be the only genuinely competitive moment of the game. Alabama gained 351 yards of total offense against Southern Cal, while holding the Trojans to only 41. Alabama earned 18 first downs, USC managed only 3. Over 60 minutes of football, Southern Cal was only able to gain 6 yards rushing—an average of 1 yard every 10 minutes of game time, or 4 feet 6 inches every quarter of play.

As a sophomore in the 1946 Rose Bowl game, Harry Gilmer almost single-handedly destroyed Southern Cal. He gained 116 yards on 16 carries and completed 4 passes for 59 yards.

In 1946, Frank Thomas coached his 15th consecutive winning season at Alabama. Under his leadership, the Crimson Tide won five SEC and two national championships. Pictured above is action from the last game Thomas coached at Legion Field, a 12–7 win over Vanderbilt.

GREATNESS LOST

(1947–1957)

By the time Frank Thomas died in 1954, Alabama's football fortunes were in decline. The championship tradition Thomas had established from the legacy bequeathed by Wallace Wade eroded during the tenure of Thomas' immediate successor, Harold "Red" Drew, who took over in 1947. Though Drew's early teams were moderately successful, he resigned following the 1954 campaign, which saw the Tide winless in its last six games, including a 28–0 loss to Auburn. The keepers of what was left of the flame of Alabama's former greatness believed that only someone who had played for both Frank Thomas and Wallace Wade could change things in Tuscaloosa.

They had no idea of the disastrous direction that change would take.

Jennings B. "Ears" Whitworth had played for Wade on the undefeated and untied 1930 Crimson Tide squad, and for Thomas on the 1931 team. As a player, Whitworth had tasted defeat only once. His pedigree, however, proved to be no guarantee of coaching success. As the head coach at Oklahoma A&M (later Oklahoma State), Whitworth not only compiled a losing record, but his 1951 team was stained by the on-field bludgeoning, widely believed to have been racially motivated, of Drake University quarterback Johnny Bright, who was African American. Bright sustained a broken jaw, and 50 years after the "Johnny Bright Incident," the OSU president issued a written apology.

Whitworth's win-loss record at Oklahoma A&M, however, is respectable compared to the wreckage over which he presided in his three ignominious years at Alabama. From 1955 to 1957, Alabama won only four football games and never more than two in any season. Whitworth was winless against perennial opponents Tennessee, Vanderbilt, and Georgia Tech. Worst of all, under Whitworth's inept coaching, Alabama lost three times to Auburn by a combined score of 100–7.

The hard-won tradition of greatness, built on the foundation laid by George Denny and achieved through the work and dedication of the athletes who played for Xen Scott, Wallace Wade, and Frank Thomas, lay in ruins by the end of 1957. The program that had led all other southern schools onto the national stage did not win a game between October 1954 and October 1956, and was so diminished by Whitworth's final season that the team was unable to score a single point in half of its games. By every meaningful measure, Alabama might as well have stopped playing college football.

Vaughn Mancha (left) was the team captain in 1947, his senior season and Red Drew's first year as head coach. Frank Thomas described Mancha as "a brilliant defensive man, fine at diagnosing plays, a great defender against passes, and a sure tackler. On offense he is a fine blocker, and a good, accurate snapper. And he loves football."

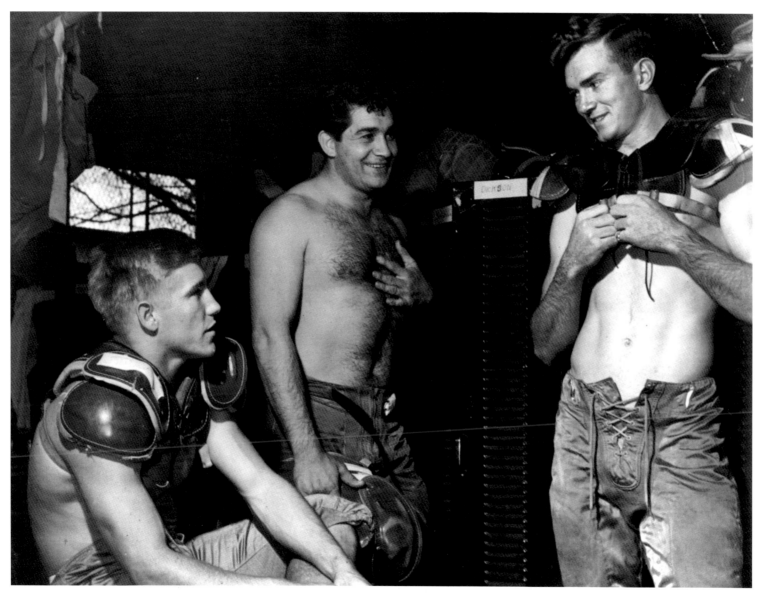

Lowell Tew, Vaughn Mancha, and Harry Gilmer were teammates for four seasons, 1944–1947. In 41 games, they and their teammates outscored all opponents 1,098 to 374. In 1947, Red Drew's inaugural year as head coach, Alabama finished the regular season with a record of 8-2 but lost to Texas in the Sugar Bowl, 27–7.

A Homecoming parade consisting of floats and marching units from all student organizations is a perennial feature of the fall celebration for returning alumni, including this one in 1948.

The Homecoming court is traditionally presented during halftime.

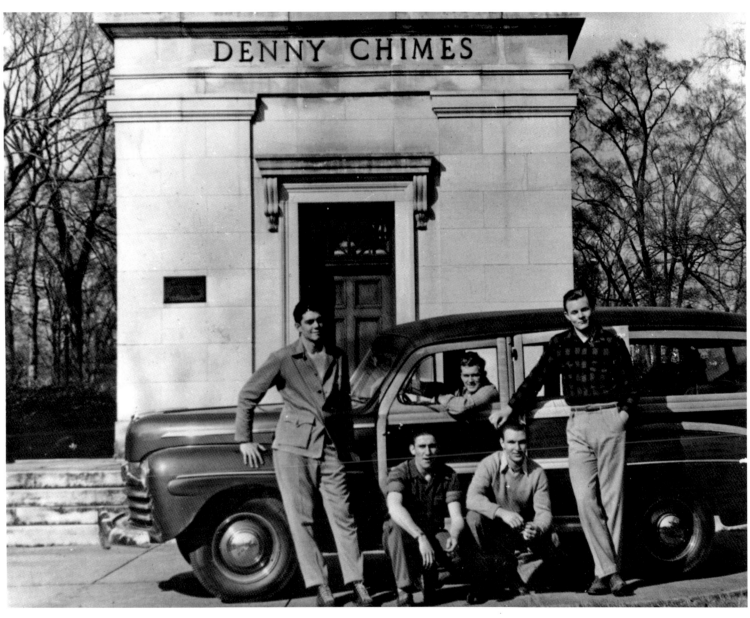

Students pose in front of Denny Chimes in the 1950s. A tribute to the man whose leadership brought the University of Alabama onto the national stage, the art-deco carillon stands 115 feet high and holds 25 bronze bells.

The Tide career record for yards per rush is held by Bobby Marlow. Over three seasons, from 1950 to 1952, he gained 2,560 yards on 408 carries, a record average of 6.3 yards per carry.

Bobby Marlow leaps a Syracuse tackler in the January 1, 1953, Orange Bowl, a resounding 61–6 victory for Alabama.

The high-water mark of the decade between the retirement of Frank Thomas and the hiring of Paul Bryant was Alabama's 61–6 crushing of Syracuse in the Orange Bowl on New Year's Day 1953. Alabama scored nine touchdowns and outgained the Orangemen 586 yards of offense to 232. Jess Richardson (68), Tommy Lewis (42), and Bobby Marlow (32) savor the victory.

Tommy Lewis (left) and Bobby Marlow combined for three of Alabama's seven offensive touchdowns against Syracuse in the 1953 Orange Bowl. Alabama's eighth TD came on a punt return, and the ninth was scored on an interception.

A traditional feature of on-campus game days is an invitation-only reception on the lawn of the President's Mansion. Guests include senior faculty, distinguished alumni, government officials, visiting dignitaries, and friends of the university.

As an assistant under Coach Frank Thomas, Red Drew was a part of five SEC and two national championships. As Alabama's head coach, even with talented players like Bobby Marlow and Bart Starr, Drew only won a single conference championship in eight seasons.

A freshman at Alabama in 1952, Bart Starr, carrying the ball, would develop into one of the finest quarterbacks ever to play the game. As a professional, coached by Vince Lombardi, he guided the Green Bay Packers to six division championships, five NFL titles, and two Super Bowl victories.

After winning the SEC championship in 1953, Alabama accepted an invitation to play Rice University in the Cotton Bowl. Shown here in Dallas are (left to right) Bill Brooks, Bart Starr, Jeff Moorer, Harry Lee, Bill "Rocky" Stone, Nick Germanos, John McBride, John Snoderly, and Bill Hollis. During the game, a 28–6 Alabama loss, the Tide's Tommy Lewis impulsively entered the field from the sidelines to tackle Rice's Dicky Moegle (later Maegle), who had broken free on a likely 95-yard touchdown run. The referee awarded a touchdown anyway, and Lewis, immediately horrified by what he had done, apologized to the Rice team both at halftime and after the game.

A future Pro Football Hall of Famer, Bart Starr played on Coach Red Drew's 1952 team that went 10-2 and defeated Syracuse in the Orange Bowl, and on the 1953 team that won the SEC championship. He played quarterback and defensive back, and also punted. Here, Starr extends for an interception against Rice in the 1954 Cotton Bowl.

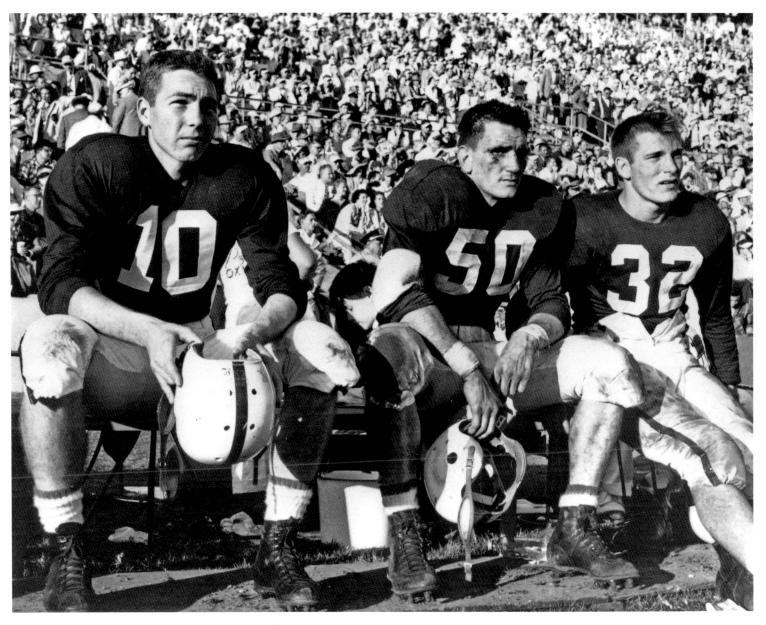

Bart Starr, Ralph Carrigan, and Bobby Marlow watch the action in 1952. In 1955, Starr's senior year at Alabama, coach J. B. Whitworth decided to implement a youth movement and relegated Starr to the bench. The Green Bay Packers drafted Starr in the 17th round. Whitworth's career record at Alabama was 4-24-2.

In 1946, bleachers were added to the end zones of Denny Stadium, and other renovations were made to expand the seating to 31,000. This rendering shows a planned further expansion designed to enlarge the capacity to 43,000.

Paul Bryant and the Return of Greatness

(1958–1969)

The second golden age of Alabama football began with a 13–3 loss to defending national champion LSU at Ladd Stadium in Mobile. This defeat was followed a week later by a scoreless tie with Vanderbilt in Birmingham. By the third game of the 1958 season, a 29–6 victory over Furman in Tuscaloosa, a trend was emerging. Whatever deficiencies Alabama might have in other phases of the game, Paul Bryant's first Alabama team played tough, stingy defense. The Tide earned a record of 5-4-1 in Bryant's inaugural season, but more important, Alabama did not allow any opponent to score more than 14 points in a game and only surrendered 75 all year.

One would have to turn the record book back at least 18 pages, to 1939, in order to find a season when Alabama had allowed fewer points. The 1959 team only surrendered 59, and the next year's team gave up only 56. In 1961, Alabama won its first of Bryant's six national championships, and the Tide outscored its 11 opponents 297–25.

During the decade of the 1960s, led by stars such as Pat Trammell, Lee Roy Jordan, Joe Namath, Steve Sloan, Kenny Stabler, and Ray Perkins, among many others, Bryant's teams averaged more than nine wins per season and claimed three national and four conference championships. Bryant matched Wallace Wade's astonishing mark of three national titles in his first eight seasons, and many remain convinced the number of national championships should have been higher, that the poll voters deprived the 1966 team of a record-setting third consecutive national title, despite the fact that Alabama was the only undefeated and untied major college program in the country.

Alabama played 26 games without a loss between October 22, 1960, and November 10, 1962. During the 1960s, Alabama played many memorable games, at least two of which have become iconic: the 1967 "Run in the Mud" game in which Stabler led Alabama over Auburn, and the 1969 "Shootout" between Scott Hunter of Alabama and Archie Manning of Ole Miss.

Most remarkable of all, the longer he coached, the more Bryant won.

Paul Bryant poses with his mid-1960s coaching staff. Bryant left a successful program and supportive fans at Texas A&M, where he was head coach, to replace J. B. Whitworth as head coach at the Capstone. When asked why he left a winning team to take over a losing one, Bryant said, "Mama called."

Bryant's players carry him from the field in triumph after beating Auburn 3–0 in 1960. It was once said of Bryant that "he could take his players and beat yours, and then take yours and beat his."

Denny Stadium is shown from above after completion in 1961 of renovations that allowed the on-campus facility to hold 43,000. Five years and three national championships later, Denny Stadium would be enlarged again.

Bryant recruited his first freshman class by promising the players they would win a national championship at Alabama if they "hung in there." By their senior year, 1961, Bryant's prediction had been made reality.

The defensive leader of the 1961 senior class was Billy Neighbors (center). Alabama's opponents only scored 25 points all season. The Tide defense shut out its last five regular season opponents and never gave up more than 7 points in any game. Billy Neighbors was one of five Bryant players to be inducted into the College Football Hall of Fame.

Pat Trammell, shown here consulting with Coach Bryant, quarterbacked the 1961 national championship team through a perfect 11-0 season. He was named the SEC Most Valuable Player and was voted Collegiate Player of the Year by the Touchdown Club of Atlanta.

Bryant once said of quarterback Pat Trammell, "He can't run and he can't throw. All he can do is beat you." Trammell died of cancer at the age of 28. Bryant wrote of Trammell's death, "It was the saddest day of my life."

President John F. Kennedy (speaking on telephone) attended the 1961 National Football Foundation Hall of Fame dinner honoring Alabama's national championship. The dinner was held December 6, 1961, in New York City.

The MacArthur Trophy, symbolic of the national championship since 1959, was presented to Coach Bryant (left) and Pat Trammell (center) after the 1961 season by General Douglas MacArthur (right), for whom the trophy is named.

Pooley Hubert (left) ignited the Tide's third quarter explosion in the 1926 Rose Bowl. He gained 97 of the Tide's 220 rushing yards and completed four passes for 141 yards and a touchdown. In his playing career at Alabama, he scored 35 touchdowns, and in six different games he scored at least three TDs. Wallace Wade said, "Pooley was the greatest team leader and playmaker that I ever coached." Here, during a 1964 game in Tuscaloosa, Hubert is recognized for his induction into the College Football Hall of Fame.

Jim Goostree (center) served as head athletic trainer at Alabama the entire time Paul Bryant was head football coach. In 1995 he was inducted into the Alabama Athletic Trainers Association Hall of Fame.

On November 17, 1962, Alabama's 26-game winning streak ended with a one point loss to Georgia Tech in Atlanta. The Tide rebounded with two decisive shutouts: a 38–0 trouncing of Auburn on December 1, and a 17–0 Orange Bowl win over Oklahoma on January 1, 1963. This action, with Alabama on offense, is during the Orange Bowl victory.

Florida defeated Alabama 10–6 on October 12, 1963, at Denny Stadium. Here, an Alabama player picks up hard-earned yardage in the losing effort. The Gators would be the last visiting team for 20 years to leave Tuscaloosa with a victory, as Bryant's teams compiled a record of 52 consecutive on-campus wins.

In Lee Roy Jordan's three varsity years, Alabama's record was 29-2-2. Bryant said of Jordan, "He was one of the finest football players the world has ever seen. If runners stayed between the sidelines he tackled them. He never had a bad day. He was 100 percent every day in practice and in the games."

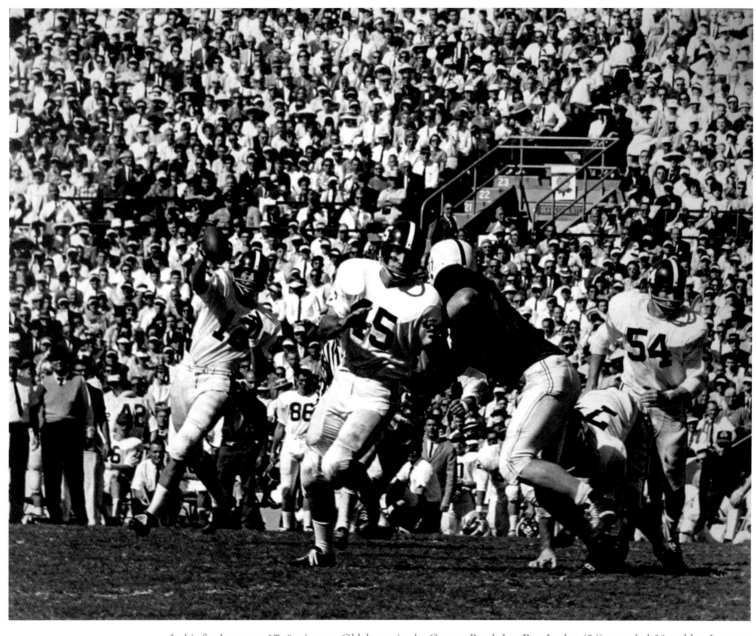

In his final game, a 17–0 win over Oklahoma in the Orange Bowl, Lee Roy Jordan (54) recorded 30 tackles. Later an All-Pro linebacker with the Dallas Cowboys, he played both offense and defense at Alabama and was inducted into the College Football Hall of Fame in 1983.

In the three years
Joe Namath played
quarterback at Alabama,
the Tide's record was
29–4, with a national
championship in 1964,
Namath's senior season.
Drafted by the St. Louis
Cardinals of the National
Football League and
the New York Jets of
the American Football
League, the star Alabama
quarterback shocked the
football world by choosing
the Jets of the upstart AFL.

Coach Bryant was once asked what he would have done if Joe Namath had been his quarterback in the wishbone offenses of the 1970s. "We would have added another row of lights on the scoreboard," Bryant replied.

Namath's favorite target at Alabama was wide receiver Ray Perkins.

Over the 1964 and 1965 seasons, Alabama won back-to-back national championships and compiled a record of 19-2-1, including this 17–9 win over LSU in Birmingham on November 7, 1964. Steve Sloan is the ball carrier.

The national anthem before the Homecoming game is traditionally played by Million Dollar Band alumni attending their class reunion, as here in 1964.

In the 1965 season, the Alabama quarterbacks, including senior Steve Sloan (14) and sophomore Kenny Stabler (12), completed 58.2 percent of all their pass attempts.

144

Steve Sloan takes instruction from Coach Bryant during the Orange Bowl on New Year's Day 1966. Alabama entered the Orange Bowl ranked fourth in the polls and beat Nebraska handily, 39–28. Every higher-ranked team either lost its bowl game or did not play, and Bryant won his third national championship.

Steve Sloan (14) completed a 32-yard touchdown pass to Ray Perkins for Alabama's first score against Nebraska in the 1966 Orange Bowl.

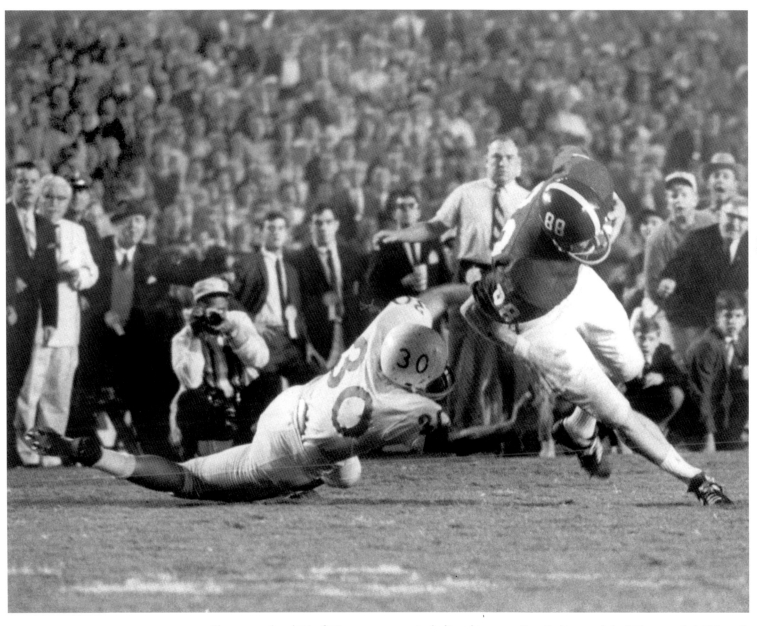

Sloan completed 20 of 29 pass attempts, including this one to Ray Perkins, and the Tide compiled 518 yards of total offense on its way to beating the Cornhuskers in the 1966 Orange Bowl.

In the early 1960s, even Bryant's assistant coaches wore ties on the sidelines during games, including defensive assistant head coach Ken Donahue (seated).

During his professional career, after stardom at Alabama, the left-handed passer Kenny Stabler would lead the Oakland Raiders through much of the 1970s, including Oakland's victory over Minnesota in the 1977 Super Bowl.

Following Spread: This aerial view shows Denny Stadium after renovations in 1966 increased the seating capacity to 59,000. This would be the last expansion of the home field for 22 years. In 1988, an upper deck would be added to the west side.

Alabama's perfect season of 1966 was nearly ruined on this third Saturday in October. With the team trailing 10–8 in the fourth quarter, Kenny Stabler (12) directed a magnificent, 14-play drive to the Tennessee 1-yard line. There, on fourth down, Steve Davis kicked the game-winning field goal.

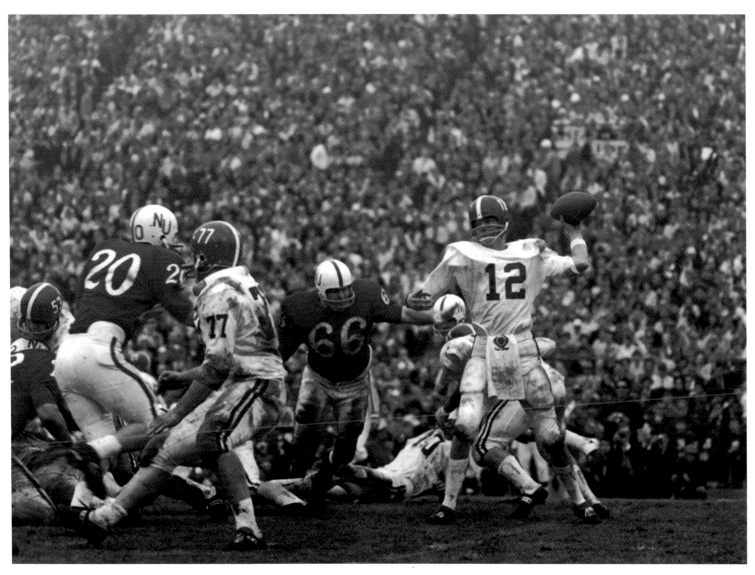

Alabama and Nebraska met for a rematch, in the Sugar Bowl, a year and a day after the Tide defeated the Cornhuskers in the 1966 Orange Bowl to clinch an improbable national championship. The undefeated defending champions from Alabama destroyed Nebraska 34–7 in the Sugar Bowl, a game that saw the Tide gain 436 yards total offense, score in every quarter, and intercept the Cornhuskers five times.

Kenny Stabler, his nickname "Snake" emblazoned on a pad, talks with teammates during the 1967 Sugar Bowl win. The poll voters awarded the 1966 national championship to Notre Dame, which had played for a 10–10 tie against Michigan State during the regular season and did not play in a bowl game. Michigan State was given the second-place ranking, though the Spartans did not play in a bowl game either. The victorious defending national champions were consigned to third place in the final poll. Thus was Coach Bryant denied the distinction of having coached a team to three consecutive national titles.

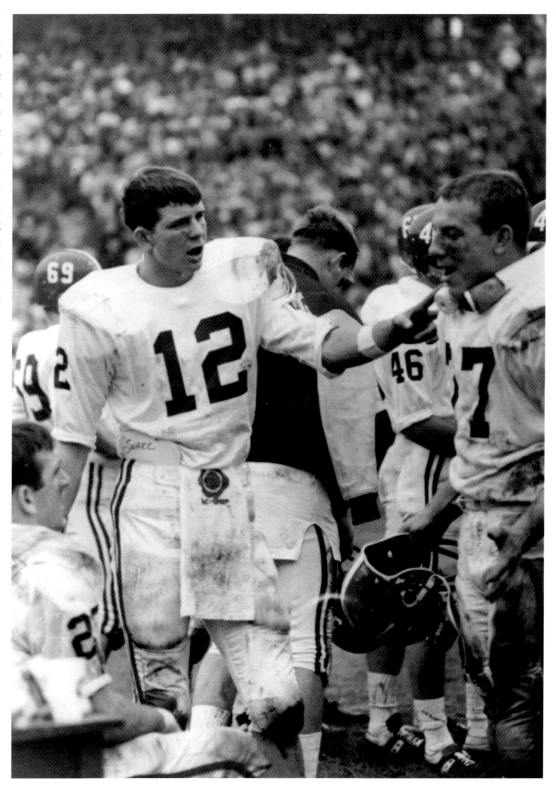

Ray Perkins was the favorite receiver of three great Alabama quarterbacks: Joe Namath, Steve Sloan, and Kenny Stabler. During Perkins' varsity career, Alabama's record was 29-2-1.

Paul Bryant's famous coaching tower. From this perch he observed the assistant coaches putting their players through drills in practice. Neither players nor coaches wanted to give Bryant any reason to come down from his tower in order to make a correction.

A Legacy of Greatness

(1970–1983)

The decade of the 1970s would witness one of the greatest 10-year runs by any college football program, as Tide players became the first collegians to win more than 100 games in a 10-year span. A great accomplishment in its own right, it is even more astonishing given that Alabama began its run in 1970 by losing to Southern California 42–21 in front of a capacity crowd at Birmingham's Legion Field, and posted a season record of only 6-5. But the next season, Alabama paid a return visit to Los Angeles and unveiled Bryant's version of the wishbone offense. Over the remainder of the decade, Alabama would win eight SEC championships and three national titles.

The 1970 thrashing by USC, which included Sam Cunningham and a number of other African Americans on the squad, was the first integrated college game ever played in Alabama. But by the time that game was played, Wilbur Jackson had become the first African American to receive a football scholarship to the university, and in 1971 John Mitchell would become the first African American to start for the Tide. Overall, under Bryant, the decade of the 1970s was filled with dominating players such as College Football Hall of Fame member Johnny Musso, Pro Football Hall of Fame member Dwight Stephenson, and Ozzie Newsome and John Hannah, who earned places in both Halls.

Coach Bryant's 25-year tenure was not without controversy. Detractors accused him of promoting dirty play. The *Saturday Evening Post* defamed Bryant and Georgia coach Wally Butts with a fabricated charge of game-fixing. And as the civil rights movement gained strength through the 1960s, the Alabama football program was increasingly criticized for having no black players. It has been theorized the denial of a national championship to Bryant's 1966 team was a judgment based on politics rather than accomplishment. Yet despite controversy and the tumultuous changes that rocked the country during the 1960s and 1970s, for fans of the Crimson Tide there was one great, unassailable constant—the supremacy of Alabama football.

Under Bryant, the Crimson Tide righted the scales with its greatest rivals, defeating Tennessee 16 times and Auburn 20 times, including on November 28, 1981, Bryant's record-setting 315th career victory. Paul Bryant coached his final game on December 29, 1982, a win over Illinois in the Liberty Bowl. When asked what he would do if he didn't coach football, Bryant once quipped, "I'd probably croak in a week." He missed his prediction by 21 days.

In the opening game of the 1971 season, Alabama traveled to Los Angeles and avenged its 1970 home opening loss to Southern Cal. Johnny Musso, shown leaning for yardage, scored two touchdowns in the first half, and Alabama, employing its new wishbone offense, punished the Trojans by gaining 302 yards rushing in a 17–10 victory.

The wishbone offense demands excellent offensive-line play. Perhaps the finest offensive lineman ever to wear the Alabama uniform, John Hannah (left) is one of only three players from the school to be elected to membership in both the College Football Hall of Fame and the Pro Football Hall of Fame (Don Hutson and Ozzie Newsome are the other two). Here, Hannah and teammates Jim Krapf, Doug Faust, and Jeff Rouzie (left to right) give their undivided attention to assistant coach Pat Dye.

On its way to an undefeated 1971 regular season, Alabama defeated Tennessee 32–15 on the third Saturday in October, the first of 11 straight victories over the Volunteers. Here, Johnny Musso and a pair of UT players shake hands after the game.

Alabama capped the 1971 season with a crushing 31–7 defeat of Auburn. The Tide gained 400 yards of total offense, including the yardage fought for here by Johnny Musso, while holding the Tigers to only 178. The 1971 SEC championship would be Alabama's first of five consecutive league championships and the first of eight conference titles it would win during the decade of the 1970s.

Johnny Musso stood only
5 feet 11 inches tall, and
his playing weight was only
194 pounds, but he was
described as "a bulldozing
blocker and breakaway
runner."

Johnny Musso, a classic overachiever, was one of Coach Bryant's favorite players. He led the SEC in rushing in 1970 and 1971, and also in scoring (100 points) in 1971. He set a school record for rushing touchdowns (34) that lasted for 28 years.

Johnny Musso (center) enjoys a laugh with Joe Namath and Paul Bryant during a postseason fete. Following his senior year, Musso finished fourth in Heisman Trophy voting and was named player of the year by *Football News,* the Miami Touchdown Club, and the Touchdown Club of Atlanta. He was inducted into the College Football Hall of Fame in 2000.

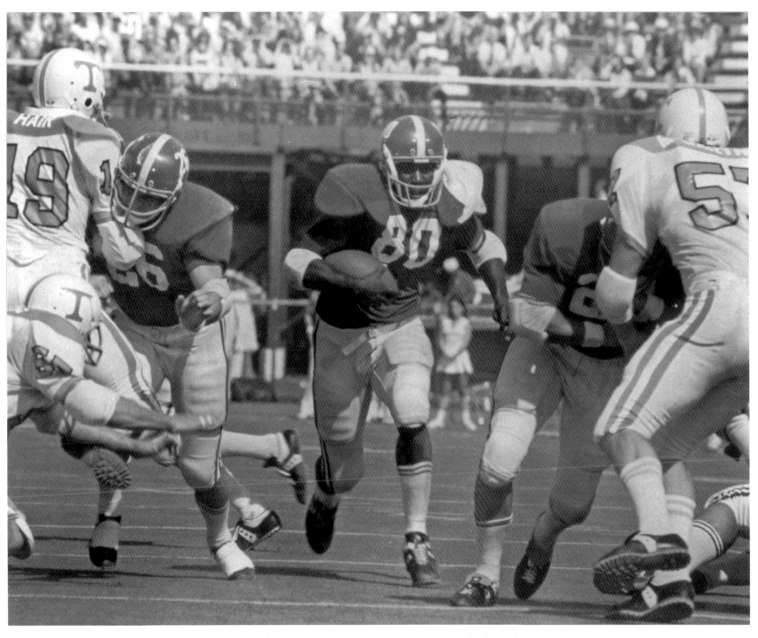

As a high school senior in 1969, Wilbur Jackson (80) of Ozark, Alabama, became the first African American to receive a football scholarship to the University of Alabama. He was recruited to play receiver, but after Coach Bryant installed the wishbone offense, Jackson was moved to running back. In 1973, his senior season, Alabama won the national championship, and Jackson rushed for an average 7.9 yards per carry.

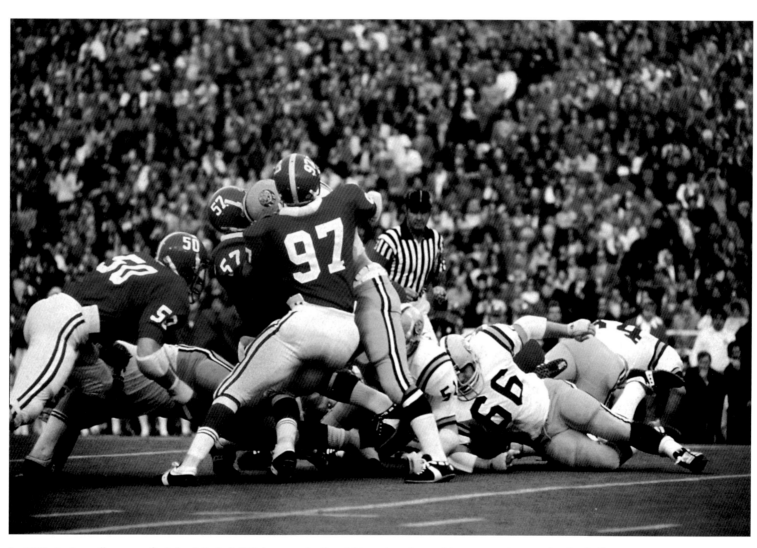

In 1971, junior college transfer John Mitchell (97) became the first African American athlete to start in a varsity football game for the Crimson Tide. After his stellar career at the Capstone, Mitchell played and coached in the NFL.

Linebacker Woodrow Lowe (47) is the only Bryant-era player to be named first-team All-American each of his three varsity years (1973-75). Each of those years, Alabama won the SEC championship. In the national championship year of 1973, Lowe set the Alabama record for most tackles in a season—134.

A future Pro Football Hall of Fame member, Ozzie Newsome (82) was a four-year starter for the Crimson Tide. During his varsity career, Alabama won three SEC championships.

Ozzie Newsome set a conference record by averaging 20.3 yards per reception. Alabama's record while Newsome played was 42-6 and included bowl game wins over Penn State, UCLA, and Ohio State.

Coach Bryant said that Ozzie Newsome was "the greatest end in Alabama history and that includes Don Hutson."

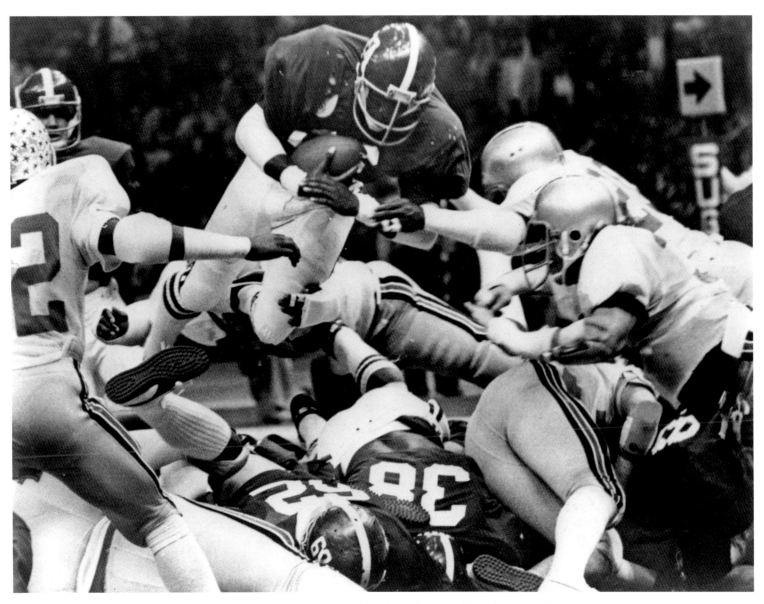

Alabama lost the second game of the 1977 regular season 31–24 to Nebraska. Otherwise, the Tide outscored its opponents 380–139, including a 35–6 trouncing of Ohio State in the Sugar Bowl. Tony Nathan, vaulting the pile, scored Alabama's first touchdown against the Buckeyes.

Alabama gained 286 yards rushing against a Buckeye defense that had shut out four of its regular season opponents and held three other teams to seven points or less.

Besides scoring the first touchdown, Tony Nathan caught a Jeff Rutledge pass for a two-point conversion in the third quarter of the 1978 Sugar Bowl against Ohio State.

Big-name entertainment has become a mainstay of activities surrounding Homecoming weekend. Enjoying the 1979 Homecoming game, Bob Hope is flanked by university president David Matthews (far right) and wife Mary Matthews.

Coach Bryant in his signature checkered hat.

Dwight Stephenson (57) played center on the 1978 and 1979 national championship teams. He was named All-American his junior and senior seasons and was drafted by Miami in the second round of the 1980 NFL draft. He played for eight seasons in the NFL and was selected All-Pro five consecutive times. He was inducted into the Pro Football Hall of Fame in 1998.

Alabama's victory over Florida in November 1978 was typical of Bryant's wishbone teams. The Tide compiled 496 yards of total offense, 23 first downs, and 23 points. The Alabama defense, including Marty Lyons (93), smothered the Gators, holding Florida to 194 yards and 8 first downs, while forcing 4 fumbles.

Assistant coach Mal Moore, later Alabama's athletic director, discusses offensive strategy with quarterbacks Steadman Shealy (10) and Jeff Rutledge (11), and running back Lou Ikner (30). Shealy and Rutledge quarterbacked the Tide to consecutive SEC and national championships in 1978 and 1979, the last national titles of the Bryant era.

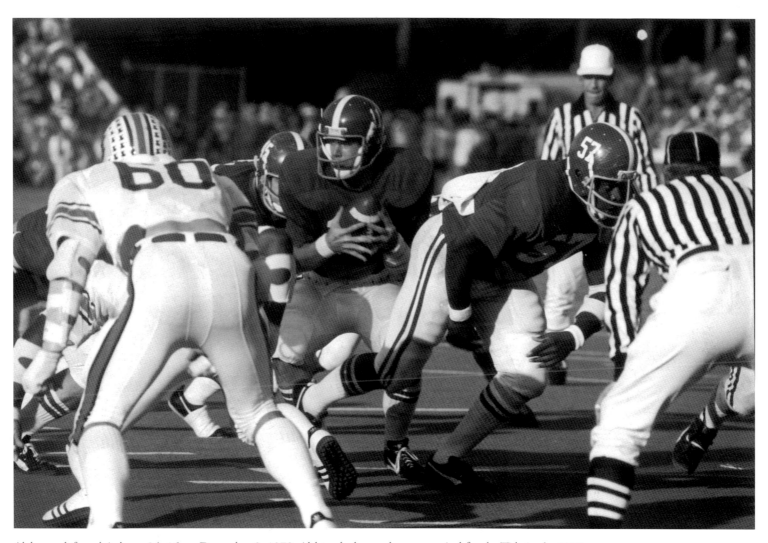

Alabama defeated Auburn 34–16 on December 2, 1978. Although the results were typical for the Tide in the 1970s, the way Alabama scored was not. Jeff Rutledge, quarterback of the run-oriented Alabama offense, completed 13 of 21 pass attempts for 174 yards and three touchdowns. Here, Dwight Stephenson leads the blocking for Rutledge.

Don McNeal was a three-year starter at defensive back, 1977-79, and played on Alabama teams that compiled a combined record of 34-2.

Don McNeal heads upfield against Baylor in 1979, probably after one of Alabama's six interceptions during the game. Alabama fans will always remember McNeal for his solo tackle of Penn State's Don Fitzkee on second down of the famous goal line stand in the 1979 Sugar Bowl. The fourth-quarter stand secured for Alabama a 14–7 victory and the national championship.

Don McNeal (28), David Hannah (74), and Mike Brock (70) await the coin toss. McNeal was a member of two consecutive national championship teams and was one of the team captains for the 1979 season.

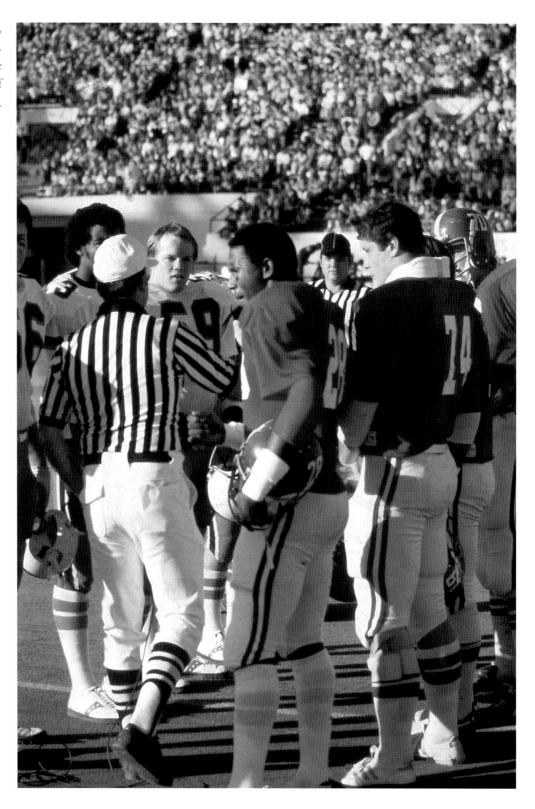

Bundled up against the weather after Alabama's 38–6 defeat of UCLA in the 1976 Liberty Bowl, Coach Bryant shares a celebratory moment with linebacker Barry Krauss, one of the most decorated defensive players of the Bryant era. Krauss was the 1976 Liberty Bowl MVP, the 1978 Sugar Bowl MVP, a three-year letterman (1976-78), a two-year All-American (1977-78), and a member of the University of Alabama All-Century Team.

Celebrating a 20–17 victory over Washington in 1978, Barry Krauss (77) was the emotional leader of the defense. He will always be remembered as the player who delivered the initial hit on fourth down to stop Penn State at the one-yard line in the goal line stand of the 1979 Sugar Bowl.

Murray Legg and E. J. Junior were part of the goal-line-stand defense that denied Penn State a potentially game-tying score in the 1979 Sugar Bowl. The two are pictured with the AP National Championship Trophy in front of Bryant Hall.

Alabama lines up in the wishbone against Penn State. Coach Bryant employed the wishbone offense to devastating effect against opposing defenses. The wishbone is a run-oriented, triple-option offense that allows the quarterback to run the option to either side of the line of scrimmage.

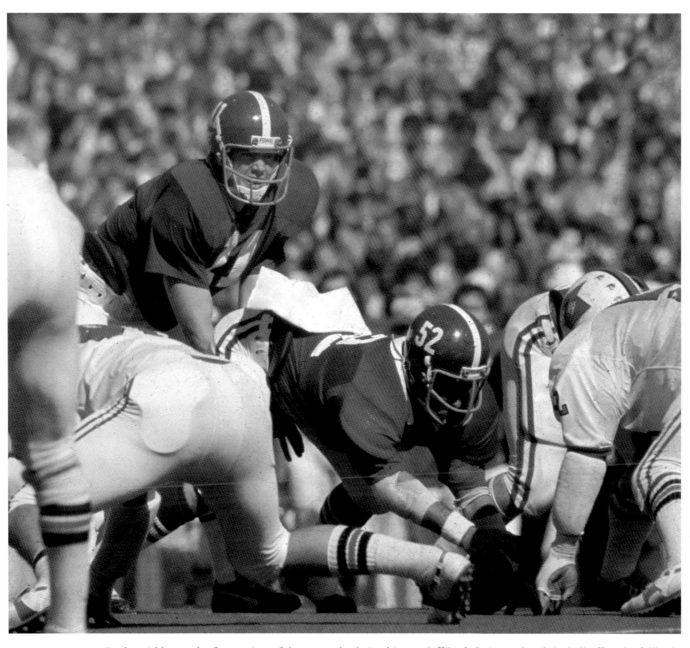

In the wishbone, the first option of the quarterback (in this case Jeff Rutledge) is to hand the ball off to the fullback. As he looks to do so, he simultaneously reads the defensive tackle or linebacker who is unblocked.

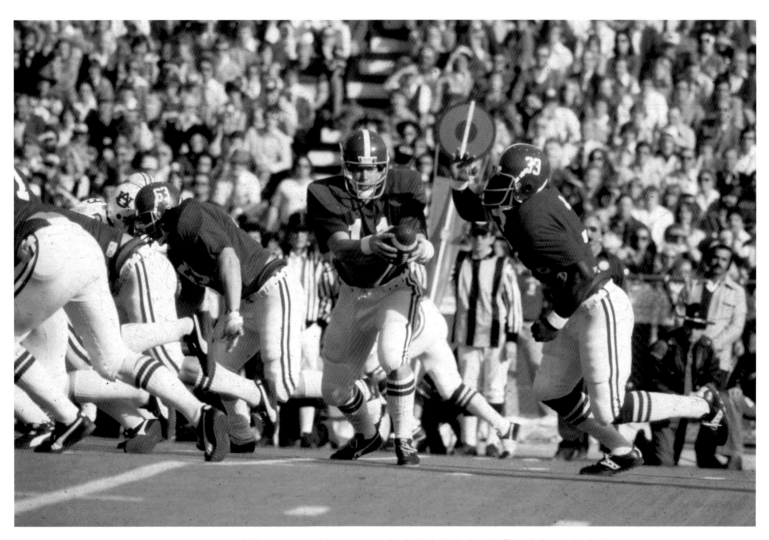

If the unblocked defender looks to tackle the fullback, the wishbone quarterback "rides" the handoff, withdraws the ball, and runs down the line of scrimmage for his second option read.

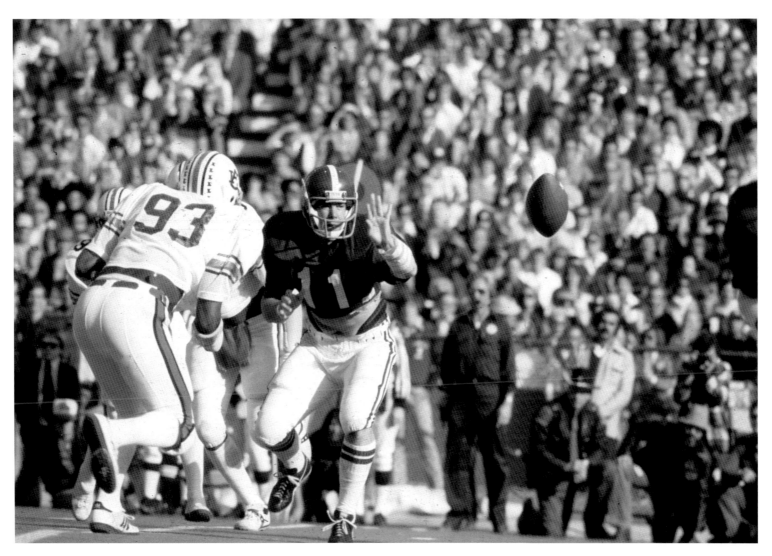

The quarterback's second option read in the wishbone is of the defensive end or outside linebacker. If the defender moves to tackle the quarterback, then the quarterback pitches the ball to the trailing running back. The lead running back's job is to block. Executed properly against the right defense, the wishbone results in the ball carrier breaking through to the defensive secondary, with the wide receiver blocking on the safety.

Assistant coach Ken Donahue supervises pregame warm-ups. Donahue was widely regarded as one of the best "working coaches" of his generation.

The immediate heir to Jeff Rutledge's spot at the point of the wishbone, Dothan native Steadman Shealy quarterbacked Alabama to the 1979 national championship.

In the 1979 season, Alabama gained 3,792 yards rushing. Nine different players rushed for more than 100 yards in the season. Quarterback Steadman Shealy led all ball carriers with 791 yards.

Although shaken up during the game against LSU in 1979, Steadman Shealy carried the ball 25 times, the most rush attempts by an Alabama player in any game that season.

Alabama scored 45 rushing touchdowns during the 1979 season. Shealy scored 11 of them, including this one in the fourth quarter from the Auburn eight-yard line to erase a one-point deficit and complete an undefeated regular season.

Coach Bryant's sixth national championship—Alabama's eleventh—was cemented with a 24–9 defeat of Arkansas in the Sugar Bowl on New Year's Day 1980. Alabama had 284 yards rushing, and Shealy completed 4 of 7 pass attempts for 70 yards.

Coach Bryant's record-setting 315th coaching victory came on November 29, 1981, when Alabama defeated Auburn, coached by Bryant's former coaching pupil Pat Dye, 28–17 in the Iron Bowl.

Walter Lewis (right) started at quarterback during Coach Bryant's final two seasons. As a senior in 1983, he and teammate Randy Edwards were elected team captains. Their handprints and those of all other football captains are preserved in concrete at the base of Denny Chimes.

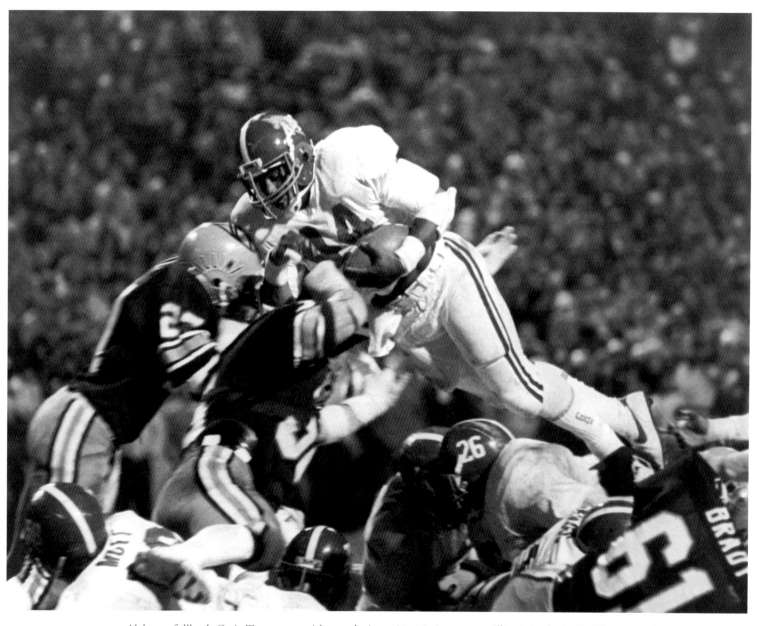

Alabama fullback Craig Turner goes airborne during a 21–15 victory over Illinois in the 1982 Liberty Bowl, the final game of Alabama's second golden age.

"If you believe in yourself, have dedication and pride and never quit, you'll be a winner."

—*Paul W. Bryant*

Fireworks over Bryant-Denny Stadium light the campus, with Denny Chimes aglow at right. "The price of victory is high, but so are the rewards," wrote Paul Bryant, player (1932-35), assistant coach (1936-40), and head football coach (1958-82) at the University of Alabama.

EPILOGUE

In 2006, the University of Alabama completed another major renovation of its on-campus coliseum, now named Bryant-Denny Stadium, and within three years, work began on a final phase of expansion to increase the seating capacity to a number almost ten times greater than that of the 12,000-seat arena built by George Denny. The 2006 makeover included new locker rooms, new amenities for the fans, and a splendid avenue for pedestrians stretching south from University Boulevard to a newly designed main entrance on the north end of the stadium itself. This broad walkway, named the Walk of Champions, is paved with large granite slabs commemorating each of the Tide's conference and national championships. Along the western edge of the Walk stand four larger-than-life statues of the men who have coached the Crimson Tide to its national championships. Each statue stands on a low pedestal inside its own curved balustrade, on which are etched the years that the respective coaches won their national titles. The statue of Wallace Wade stands closest to University Boulevard. Frank Thomas' statue is next to Wade's and is followed by that of Paul Bryant. The statue of Gene Stallings, whose 1992 squad won Alabama's 12th national championship, is closest to the stadium.

On the southern end of the Walk of Champions, next to the statue of Gene Stallings, the university has confidently left room for the statue of its next championship coach.

NOTES ON THE PHOTOGRAPHS

These notes, listed by page number, attempt to include all aspects known of the photographs. Each of the photographs is identified by the page number, photograph's title or description, photographer and collection, archive, and call or box number when applicable. Although every attempt was made to collect all data, in some cases complete data may be unavailable due to the age and condition of some of the photographs and records.

71 **FRED SINGTON DRIVING**
Paul W. Bryant Museum,
The University of Alabama
PH5954

72 **FOUR-YEAR LETTERMAN**
Paul W. Bryant Museum,
The University of Alabama
PH5949

73 **PHI BETA KAPPA**
Paul W. Bryant Museum,
The University of Alabama
PH02861

74 **SINGTON IN SWEATER**
Paul W. Bryant Museum,
The University of Alabama
PH5955

75 **WADE AND THOMAS**
Paul W. Bryant Museum,
The University of Alabama
PH00884

76 **THOMAS' FIRST TEAM**
Paul W. Bryant Museum,
The University of Alabama
PH05948

77 **JOHNNY "HURRI" CAIN**
Paul W. Bryant Museum,
The University of Alabama
PH04747

78 **JOHNNY CAIN**
Paul W. Bryant Museum,
The University of Alabama
PH01260

79 **HOWELL, HOLLY,
WALKER, CAIN**
Paul W. Bryant Museum,
The University of Alabama
PH102

80 **THOMAS, HUTSON,
HOWELL**
Paul W. Bryant Museum,
The University of Alabama
PH05983

81 **DIXIE HOWELL**
Paul W. Bryant Museum,
The University of Alabama
PH09266

82 **DIXIE HOWELL SCORING**
Paul W. Bryant Museum,
The University of Alabama

83 **RETURN CELEBRATION**
Paul W. Bryant Museum,
The University of Alabama
28383

84 **DON HUTSON**
Paul W. Bryant Museum,
The University of Alabama
PH143

85 **PAUL BRYANT**
Paul W. Bryant Museum,
The University of Alabama
PH175

86 **SUCCESSFUL PUPIL**
Paul W. Bryant Museum,
The University of Alabama
PH478

87 **1934 OFFENSIVE LINE**
Paul W. Bryant Museum,
The University of Alabama
PH1418

88 **RILEY SMITH**
Paul W. Bryant Museum,
The University of Alabama
PH01445

89 **RONALD REAGAN AND
ALABAMA PLAYERS**
Paul W. Bryant Museum,
The University of Alabama
PH01806

90 **HOLT RAST**
Paul W. Bryant Museum,
The University of Alabama
PH05008

91 **HOLT RAST #2**
Paul W. Bryant Museum,
The University of Alabama
PH05005

92 **HOLT RAST #3**
Paul W. Bryant Museum,
The University of Alabama
PH01176

93 **ELEPHANTS**
The W. S. Hoole Special
Collections Library,
The University of Alabama
2007_001_003247

94 **NELSON, THOMAS, RAST**
Paul W. Bryant Museum,
The University of Alabama

95 **GILMER, THOMAS,
MANCHA**
Paul W. Bryant Museum,
The University of Alabama
PH00435

96 **VAUGHN MANCHA**
Paul W. Bryant Museum,
The University of Alabama
PH529

97 **HARRY GILMER**
Paul W. Bryant Museum,
The University of Alabama
PH01289

98 **GILMER RUSHING**
Paul W. Bryant Museum,
The University of Alabama
PH01279

100 **BOWL SELECTION**
Paul W. Bryant Museum,
The University of Alabama
PH05010

101 **ROSE BOWL FESTIVITIES**
Paul W. Bryant Museum,
The University of Alabama
PH436

102 **ROSE BOWL COIN TOSS**
Paul W. Bryant Museum,
The University of Alabama
PH05016

103 **ROSE BOWL STAR**
Paul W. Bryant Museum,
The University of Alabama

104 **VERSUS VANDERBILT**
Paul W. Bryant Museum,
The University of Alabama
PH05015

106 **TEAM CAPTAIN MANCHA**
Paul W. Bryant Museum,
The University of Alabama
PH05011

107 **TEW, MANCHA, GILMER**
Paul W. Bryant Museum,
The University of Alabama
PH05017

108 **HOMECOMING PARADE**
The W. S. Hoole Special
Collections Library,
The University of Alabama
2007_001_002905

110 **HOMECOMING COURT**
The W. S. Hoole Special
Collections Library,
The University of Alabama
2007_001_002368

111 **PARKED BY DENNY
CHIMES**
Paul W. Bryant Museum,
The University of Alabama
PH431

112 **BOBBY MARLOW**
Paul W. Bryant Museum,
The University of Alabama
PH1419

113 **MARLOW LEAPS**
Paul W. Bryant Museum,
The University of Alabama
PH1151